UNITED WE STAND
THEN AND NOW

Abdo & Daughters
MIDDLE GRADE NONFICTION
An imprint of Abdo Publishing
abdobooks.com

Jessica Rusick

ABDOBOOKS.COM

Published by Abdo Publishing, a division of ABDO, PO Box 398166, Minneapolis, Minnesota 55439. Copyright © 2021 by Abdo Consulting Group, Inc. International copyrights reserved in all countries. No part of this book may be reproduced in any form without written permission from the publisher. Abdo & Daughters™ is a trademark and logo of Abdo Publishing.

Printed in the United States of America, North Mankato, Minnesota.

102020

012021

THIS BOOK CONTAINS RECYCLED MATERIALS

Design: Kelly Doudna, Mighty Media, Inc.

Production: Mighty Media, Inc.

Editor: Liz Salzmann

Cover Photographs: Mark Lennihan/AP Images (right), Mary Altaffer/AP Images

Interior Photographs: Beth A. Keiser/AP Images, p. 29; David Iliff, License CC BY-SA 3.0/ Wikimedia Commons, pp. 16, 17; Don Halasy/Flickr, pp. 8, 9; Energetic Communications/Flickr, p. 18; Fred Chartrand/AP Images, pp. 22, 23; Jason Kelly/Flickr, p. 42; Library of Congress/ Flickr, p. 11; Mark Lennihan/AP Images, p. 1 (right); Mary Altaffer/AP Images, p. 1; Norbert Aepli/Wikimedia Commons, p. 12; Richard Drew/AP Images, p. 14; Sgt. James K. McCann/ Flickr, pp. 38, 39; Shutterstock Images, pp. 15, 26, 27, 30, 31, 32, 33, 34, 35, 37, 41 (top), 44, 45; Steve Ludlum/Flickr, pp. 4, 5; Tara Molle/DHS Official Photographer/Flickr, p. 7; Todd Plitt/ Flickr, p. 41; US Customs and Border Protection/Flickr, p. 20; US Embassy Jerusalem/Flickr, p. 24

Design Elements: Shutterstock Images

LIBRARY OF CONGRESS CONTROL NUMBER: 2020940237

PUBLISHER'S CATALOGING-IN-PUBLICATION DATA

Names: Rusick, Jessica, author.

Title: United we stand: then and now / by Jessica Rusick

Other title: then and now

Description: Minneapolis, Minnesota : Abdo Publishing, 2021 | Series: The 9/11 terrorist attacks | Includes online resources and index

Identifiers: ISBN 9781532194528 (lib. bdg.) | ISBN 9781098213886 (ebook)

Subjects: LCSH: September 11 Terrorist Attacks, 2001--Juvenile literature. | Acts of terrorism-- Juvenile literature. | Disaster relief--Juvenile literature. | United States--History--Juvenile literature

Classification: DDC 973.931--dc23

TABLE OF CONTENTS

The September 11, 2001, plane crashes into the WTC created such great destruction that astronauts aboard the International Space Station could see smoke from the site.

Chapter 1

TERRORISTS ATTACK THE UNITED STATES

On September 11, 2001, the United States faced one of the most serious crises in its history. That morning, 19 terrorists hijacked four US commercial airplanes in midflight. Then, they steered the planes toward US landmarks. At 8:46 a.m., the first plane crashed into the North Tower of the World Trade Center (WTC) complex in New York City. Less the twenty minutes later, the second plane crashed into the South Tower of the WTC. These 110-story buildings stood right next to each other. Together, they were known as the Twin Towers.

At 9:37 a.m., the third plane crashed into the Pentagon in Washington, DC. Part of the building later collapsed. The Twin Towers had also been weakened by the crashes. At 9:59 a.m., the South Tower collapsed. Millions of pounds of steel, concrete, and other debris rained to the ground in seconds. At 10:28 a.m., the North Tower collapsed.

The fourth hijacked plane didn't reach its intended target. Some of the passengers and crew stormed the cockpit to fight the hijackers. After a struggle, the hijacker piloting the plane decided to crash the plane rather than let the passengers and crew regain control of it. The plane crashed in a field near Shanksville, Pennsylvania.

Who Was Behind the 9/11 Terrorist Attacks?

Within days after the attacks, US intelligence officials confirmed the hijackers were members of al-Qaeda. Al-Qaeda is an Islamist terrorist group based in Afghanistan. One of the group's goals is to create governments in the Middle East that enforce strict laws based on an extreme interpretation of Islam.

Al-Qaeda members believe Western countries have too much influence in the Middle East and interfere with this goal. And, they see the United States as the most influential of the Western countries. So, al-Qaeda considers the United States its enemy and uses terrorism to fight it.

However, while al-Qaeda's leaders and members believe they are acting in accordance with Islam, most Muslims disagree. They believe that al-Qaeda's beliefs and actions violate the Islamic faith, especially when al-Qaeda calls for violence against others.

Honoring Victims and Survivors

Together, the four September 11, 2001, plane hijackings by al-Qaeda members are known as the 9/11 terrorist attacks. They killed 2,977 people. The victims included office workers, first

The 9/11 Memorial at Ground Zero is decorated with flags and flowers for the 2019 tribute to the victims of the 9/11 terrorist attacks. A special ceremony has been held at Ground Zero every year since 2002.

responders, and everyone aboard the airplanes. Many Americans were angered and saddened by the attacks. Many also felt a need to help. Some people donated money and supplies, and others offered emotional support. Their actions helped the nation heal from the attacks. Years later, these charitable actions continue. Today, 9/11 charities, ceremonies, memorials, and museums show that the nation will forever be united in remembering the 9/11 terrorist attacks.

The collapse of the Twin Towers covered the surrounding blocks with ash and dust. People helped one another get safely out of the area.

Chapter 2

PULLING TOGETHER FOR NEW YORK CITY

The 9/11 terrorist attacks occurred as thousands of people had already begun filling the WTC for the day's work. The complex held restaurants, a hotel, law and financial offices, and other businesses. After the planes crashed into the WTC, these workers began evacuating from the Twin Towers. People in other nearby buildings began evacuating too. When the Twin Towers fell, the crash sent huge clouds of dust down nearby streets for blocks. Evacuees and bystanders were covered in this thick, choking dust as they tried to get to safety.

Emergency responders arrived on scene within minutes of the plane crashes. In the coming hours, many civilians helped these police officers, firefighters, and medical staff rescue and tend to victims. Nearby business owners helped too. One was Yong Lee, who owned Fulton Supply Hardware Store near the WTC. He posted a sign offering free cell phones for people to call their families. He also gave protective masks and respirators to those walking through the choking dust.

Water Evacuation

At 11:02 a.m., New York City mayor Rudolph "Rudy" Giuliani ordered people to evacuate Lower Manhattan. This is the area of the city where the WTC was located. Manhattan is an island surrounded by three rivers. Many streets, bridges, and tunnels out of the area were closed or blocked by debris. So, many people were forced to evacuate by boat.

Boats of every description pulled up along the riverbanks to help people leave Manhattan. These included fishing boats, tour boats, ferries, and US Coast Guard vessels. Over nine hours following the attacks, these boats carried nearly 500,000 civilian passengers out of Manhattan. This was the largest water evacuation in US history.

Ground Zero

Meanwhile, rescue and aid continued at the crash site for days. The WTC site became known as Ground Zero. The term *ground zero* refers to an area most affected by a disaster or attack. New York City's Ground Zero was a 16-acre (6.5 ha) pile of steel beams, glass shards, chunks of concrete, and other debris. The air was filled with dust, smoke, and toxic chemicals. Fires burned deep within the rubble pile for 100 days.

Firefighters, police officers, construction crews, and other workers began the difficult task of clearing the wreckage from

Firefighters combat WTC flames on September 11. That day, 343 firefighters died during evacuations and rescue attempts at the WTC.

Ground Zero. Many worked 12-hour shifts. The job was dangerous. It was also heartbreaking. Fewer than 20 people were found alive in the rubble. As cleanup wore on, workers recovered nearly 300 bodies from the wreckage.

For days, people across New York City held candlelight vigils for the victims. Groups gathered to share stories about loved ones who had died or who were still missing. At Union Square Park in New York City, people wrote hopeful messages on the ground in chalk. People also left flowers, candles, US flags, and more in various locations as tributes to the victims.

Helping Workers Rest and Recover

As New York City citizens remembered victims, they also mobilized to support the workers at Ground Zero. A small church called

Officials at St. Paul's Chapel aided or housed more than 3,000 Ground Zero workers in the first three months after the attacks.

St. Paul's Chapel was located just 300 feet (91 m) from Ground Zero. Though it was close to the WTC, the church survived the collapse of the Twin Towers. St. Paul's Chapel opened its doors to Ground Zero cleanup crews. More than 5,000 volunteers at the chapel provided comfort to these workers. Chefs cooked warm meals. Medical professionals treated aches and pains that resulted from the hard, physical work of cleaning up debris.

Restaurants also opened their doors to feed hungry Ground Zero workers. On September 13, Nino's Restaurant in New York City began serving free meals to these workers. For months, Nino's served several thousand workers a day. The restaurant received money, food, and equipment donations from around the country so it could keep providing free meals. During this time, nearly 8,000 volunteers showed up to serve food and wash dishes.

Another source of food and relief for cleanup workers was the Salvation Army. The organization set up a tent near Ground Zero.

During the months of cleanup, volunteers there and at other Salvation Army sites in the area served 3 million meals to workers.

Volunteers Travel to Ground Zero

Many of the Ground Zero volunteers were local citizens. But volunteers also traveled to New York City from around the country to help. Many of these volunteers were firefighters, police officers, and construction workers. Some others were mental health professionals. These volunteers provided emotional support and counseling to Ground Zero workers.

Coal miners from Kentucky also traveled to Ground Zero to help. Their work in underground mines gave them experience in building supports to keep the piles of debris from shifting and collapsing. A building demolition expert from North Carolina also came to help workers dig through the wreckage safely.

Other volunteers provided much-needed supplies to workers. The hot, sharp rubble pile at Ground Zero caused rescue workers' clothing to get damaged and dirty quickly. They needed a constant fresh supply to continue cleanup efforts. One couple traveled from

9/11 BY THE NUMBERS

More than 10,000 people volunteered at Ground Zero during cleanup efforts.

Volunteers brought 50,000 meals donated by Louisiana restaurant The Gumbo Krewe to Ground Zero workers.

the Midwest to provide fresh clothes and boots to Ground Zero workers. The Midwest volunteers set up in an abandoned building near Ground Zero. They organized donations of work boots and other durable clothing from around the city. Then, they gave the clothes to workers.

A few miles away, the parking lot of the Jacob K. Javits Convention Center also served as a supply center for Ground Zero workers. Volunteers there organized and distributed donated clothes, equipment, and food. Donations came from across the country and some were simply addressed to "Ground Zero, New York City."

Donations

Not everyone who wanted to help after the 9/11 terrorist attacks was able to travel to the crash sites to do so. So, people found other ways to contribute.

Some people raised money for the Fire Department of the City of New York (FDNY). The attacks claimed the lives of 343 New York City firefighters who were in and near the Twin Towers when they collapsed. In addition, more than 220 FDNY trucks and other vehicles had been damaged or destroyed by fires and falling debris. As news of these losses spread across the nation, residents in other states took action. People in Louisiana raised $1.2 million to purchase new fire trucks for the FDNY. In South Carolina, students at White Knoll Middle School raised $540,000 to provide the FDNY with another new fire truck.

These efforts were only the beginning. Cleanup was a massive job that took nearly nine months. But there was also emotional and financial wreckage. People around the country continued to find ways to support those affected by the 9/11 terrorist attacks.

A fire truck damaged during Ground Zero rescue efforts is on display at the 9/11 Memorial Museum in New York City.

LONG LIVE
FREEDOM!

WC♡NY
#1
FROM CT TO

USA

I♡USA!!

Unity

GS 520

I♡USA

Peace

THIS IS A MEMORIAL FOR the
VICTIMS OF SEPTEMBER 11, 2001.

WE HOPE THAT YOU WILL TAKE
COURAGE, COMFORT & PRIDE
FROM IT.

TAKE THOSE THINGS - PLEASE
DON'T TAKE THE TILES.
NO ONE NEEDS A SOUVENIR
AT THE EXPENSE OF SOMEONE'S
MEMORY.
THANKS

PROUD TO
BE A
FIREFIGHTER

Carol From Michigan

Peace

T.C. FAITH
TRUST
PEACE
AMERICA
REMEMBER HOPE
TRUTH

BRILION WI.

2002

FLORIDA

NY

BLESS
AMERICA

Texas

Following the 9/11 terrorist attacks, many people created art to both show support for victims, rescue workers, and cleanup crews and to promote communal healing.

Chapter 3

AMERICANS DONATE

One of the easiest and most efficient ways people supported relief efforts for the 9/11 terrorist attacks was through donation. Many nonprofit organizations and charities created funds for this purpose. These organizations could then distribute the money where it would do the most good, such as paying survivors' medical bills or helping victims' families with expenses.

The New York Community Trust and the United Way of New York City together formed the September 11th Fund. This fund raised $158 million and provided grants to cover the needs of families and communities affected by the attacks. The American Red Cross Liberty Disaster Relief Fund also provided relief. This fund received almost as much in donations as the September 11th Fund.

Coca-Cola, Microsoft, General Electric, and other large companies donated millions of dollars to these two funds, as well as to many other charities. Retail giant Amazon and internet company Yahoo raised millions of dollars through their customers. The companies let users donate to several charities, such as the American Red Cross and the United Way, simply by clicking a button on the Amazon or Yahoo sites. Americans donated a total of $2.8 billion to 9/11 causes in the months after the attacks. This was the most money ever raised in the aftermath of a disaster.

Cantor Fitzgerald Relief Fund

Another major relief fund was created by a company directly affected by the attacks. Finance company Cantor Fitzgerald had its headquarters on several floors near the top of the North Tower. The plane that crashed into the building struck floors below the Cantor Fitzgerald offices. It damaged the stairwells, cutting off their escape routes. All 658 Cantor Fitzgerald employees in the office that morning died.

Lutnick gave speeches and interviews after the 9/11 terrorist attacks.

Cantor Fitzgerald CEO Howard Lutnick had been out of the office that morning. His brother, Gary, worked at the company and was in the office. Gary died in the attack. Lutnick wanted to support other Cantor Fitzgerald families who had lost loved ones. So, three days after 9/11, he and his sister Edie started the Cantor Fitzgerald Relief Fund. Money from the fund went to the families of victims employed by Cantor Fitzgerald. The fund also helped families of victims who worked for 14 other WTC companies.

For the next five years, a quarter of Cantor Fitzgerald's annual profits went into the fund. And Lutnick personally contributed $1 million to the fund. He also helped families in other ways. Lutnick had Cantor Fitzgerald employees help victims' families fill out the paperwork and applications necessary to receive other financial support. And, the families of victims who worked at Cantor Fitzgerald continued to receive the company's health insurance benefits for ten years after the attacks.

Helping Children

Hundreds of children lost parents, siblings, and other loved ones in the 9/11 terrorist attacks. Some organizations were formed specifically to meet the needs of these children. One such organization was Tuesday's Children. Founders chose this name because the 9/11 terrorist attacks occurred on a Tuesday. This charity was founded to help children and communities around the world that have been affected by acts of violence.

America's Camp was another organization dedicated to helping children affected by the 9/11 terrorist attacks. It was founded in 2002. The organization's annual summer camp provided a place for the children and siblings of 9/11's victims to meet, share their

Even children who did not experience direct loss from the 9/11 terrorist attacks felt the impact of the events. Many sent rescue workers and volunteers letters and artworks of thanks.

experiences, and have fun. The camp featured activities such as games, swimming, and dance classes. Campers also participated in memorial services and art projects to honor their lost loved ones. And, grief counselors helped campers cope with painful emotions or memories.

New York's leaders also stepped in to help children, focusing on education. New York governor George Pataki established the New York State World Trade Center Memorial Scholarship. This program gave money to families of those killed or permanently injured as a result of the 9/11 terrorist attacks. The money could be used to cover the costs of attending public and private colleges in New York.

The US Government Response

Leaders provided aid on a national level too. On September 22, 2001,

Congress created the September 11th Victim Compensation Fund (VCF). This fund gave money to people who lost family members in the attacks. These families received an average payment of more than $2 million to pay bills and other expenses. Injured survivors each received about $400,000 from the fund.

In New York, the Federal Emergency Management Agency (FEMA) joined other federal and state agencies to help people and businesses recover after the attacks. By August 2002, these agencies had provided more than $670 million in relief. FEMA also provided several resources to affected New Yorkers. Housing grants helped people repair homes near the WTC that were damaged during the attacks. The grants also helped people pay for temporary housing until the repairs were completed.

9/11 BY THE NUMBERS

Between 2001 and 2004, the VCF paid out $7 billion to more than 5,560 injured survivors and families of victims.

In addition, FEMA funded Project Liberty. This program was run by the New York State Office of Mental Health. Project Liberty treated people with mental health issues caused or made worse by the 9/11 terrorist attacks. More than 750,000 people received free counseling through the program.

Thousands of people attended a memorial outside the Parliament Buildings in Ottawa, Canada, on September 14, 2001. During the ceremony, the crowd observed three minutes of silence to honor the victims of the 9/11 terrorist attacks.

Chapter 4

SUPPORT AROUND THE WORLD

In the hours after the 9/11 terrorist attacks, President George W. Bush ordered all commercial and private flights grounded in case more hijackings were planned. Planes that were already in the air had to land at the nearest airports. For some flights, the closest airport was in Canada.

Canadian Support

After the attacks, 38 planes that had been headed for US cities from Europe had to instead land at the airport in Gander, Canada. Gander is on the island of Newfoundland off the country's east coast. About 10,000 people live there. On September 11, 2001, the town welcomed more than 6,500 airplane passengers and crew.

Gander's townspeople came together to help the people from these flights. The town didn't have enough hotel rooms for everyone. So, Gander's schools, gyms, and churches became makeshift shelters. Many locals allowed passengers to sleep and shower in their homes. Others provided food at the shelters. Local restaurants also donated meals.

For security reasons, checked luggage had to stay locked in the planes' cargo holds. So, many passengers needed clean clothes and toiletries. Local stores gave passengers and crew whatever they needed for free. And, pharmacists helped passengers get medication to replace any that were stuck on the planes.

Global Mourning

In addition to the physical support in Gander, Canada also joined several nations worldwide in mourning the 9/11 terrorist attacks. It

wasn't only Americans who were victims of the attacks. More than 90 other countries also lost citizens from the day's events. Some of these victims were traveling on the hijacked planes. Others were working in the WTC or the Pentagon when the planes struck.

In the days and weeks following the attacks, people around the world honored the victims. They left flowers,

In the years following the attacks, some countries built their own 9/11 memorials. The 9/11 Living Memorial in Jerusalem, Israel, is one such monument.

flags, and other tokens outside US embassies. In Berlin, Germany, hundreds of thousands of people gathered at a vigil on September 14, 2001, at the Brandenburg Gate to show support for the United States.

Some countries honored 9/11's victims with special ceremonies. Two days after the attacks, Queen Elizabeth II ordered that the US national anthem be played during the changing of the guard ceremony outside Buckingham Palace in London, England. Outside the palace gates, thousands gathered to watch. Many of them were Americans living or vacationing in England. As the national anthem played, some sang along and wept.

PIVOTAL PERSON: KEVIN TUERFF

Kevin Tuerff was a passenger aboard one of the flights that landed in Gander, Canada. During his four-and-a-half day stay there, Tuerff was moved by the Gander townspeople's kindness and generosity. His experiences in Gander inspired him to start Pay It Forward 9/11. This organization encourages people to do three random acts of kindness for strangers on September 11 each year. An act of kindness could be as simple as giving someone your seat on crowded bus or picking up litter. In 2016, Tuerff wrote a book about his experiences in Gander called *Channel of Peace: Stranded in Gander on 9/11*. The book also details his tips for showing kindness to strangers.

At America: A Tribute to Heroes, boxer Muhammad Ali said, "I've been a Muslim for 20 years, and I'm against killing, violence—and all Muslims are against it."

Chapter 5

CELEBRITIES COME TOGETHER

In addition to national governments and citizens worldwide mourning the 9/11 terrorist attacks, many celebrities were motivated to help survivors and victims' families. In the months following the attacks, celebrities performed in three major events to raise money for 9/11-related charities.

America: A Tribute to Heroes

On September 21, 2001, some of the world's biggest celebrities united for America: A Tribute to Heroes. The two-hour concert was recorded in three studios, in Los Angeles, California; New York City; and London. Due to security concerns, there were no live audiences at these locations.

More than 20 musicians, including singer Alicia Keys and the band U2, performed at the concert. Between songs, actors Tom Hanks and Will Smith and other celebrities shared stories of 9/11's heroes.

Boxer Muhammad Ali also took part in the show to share an important message. Because of the 9/11 terrorists' connection to Islam, Muslims faced discrimination after the attacks. Ali was a Muslim. He reminded viewers that Islam was a peaceful religion that was against killing and violence. Many Muslims around the world opposed al-Qaeda's acts of terror.

During the show, viewers were encouraged to call or go online to donate money. About 38,000 volunteers, including celebrities, answered phones and monitored online donations. The concert aired on 30 different television networks and was shown in more than 200 countries. Nearly 60 million people in the United States and around the world watched. The concert raised more than $150 million for the United Way September 11th Fund.

The Concert for New York City

Another charity concert was held October 20, 2001. Singers, actors, comedians, politicians, and other well-known figures performed in the Concert for New York City. It was held at New York City's Madison Square Garden in front of a large audience. Many in attendance were first responders and victims' families. Performers included comedian Jimmy Fallon and musicians Jay-Z and Elton John.

The Concert for New York City raised $35 million for the Robin Hood Relief Fund. This organization passed the money along to several charitable organizations. Some funds helped treat the mental and physical health of survivors, first responders, victims' families, and others affected by the attacks. Robin Hood also

helped people who were unemployed because of the attacks find new jobs. And, Robin Hood sent some money directly to victims' families to use for daily expenses. In December 2001, every 9/11 victim's family received $5,000 from the fund.

United We Stand: What More Can I Give

The day after the Concert for New York City, a benefit called United We Stand: What More Can I Give was held at RFK Stadium in Washington, DC. Music icon Michael Jackson organized the event. Actor John Stamos was the host. Besides Jackson, musical performers included the Backstreet Boys, Pink, Mýa, P. Diddy, and more. Proceeds from the concert were donated to several organizations, including the American Red Cross Liberty Relief Fund, the Salvation Army Relief Fund, and the Pentagon Relief Fund.

The Tribute in Light can be seen from up to 60 miles (97 km) away.

Chapter 6

MEMORIALS AND COMMEMORATIONS

Aiding and honoring those affected by the 9/11 terrorist attacks did not end the year the tragedy occurred. From 2001 on, people remembered and mourned the day at special events and memorials.

A commemoration is held at the WTC every September 11. Family members of those killed take turns reading the names of the 9/11 victims. Many elected officials attend as well. This annual commemoration also includes the Tribute in Light. This consists of two columns of light shining near where the Twin Towers once stood. These columns are created by 88 searchlights.

In addition to the commemoration at the WTC, many other events are held in remembrance of those affected by the 9/11 terrorist attacks. And there are also permanent memorials to victims and survivors.

The Pentagon Memorial

A total of 184 victims died in the 9/11 terrorist attack at the Pentagon. This included all 59 passengers and crew aboard the plane and 125 people in the building. The Pentagon Memorial Fund was created in 2003. The fund's goal was to build a memorial to the victims of the attack. Later, an education center to teach visitors about the events of 9/11 was also planned.

In 2008, the 9/11 Pentagon Memorial was completed. It is a two-acre (0.8 ha) field near the Pentagon. The main feature of the memorial is an arrangement of 184 small benches, one for each victim of the Pentagon attack. The benches are placed according to the age of each victim. The direction each bench faces is based

The benches at the 9/11 Pentagon Memorial are made of stainless steel and granite. Each one is inscribed with a victim's name.

on whether the victim was in the building or on the plane. Beneath each bench is a narrow pool of water that is lit up at night. Crape myrtle trees planted throughout the memorial provide shade.

The memorial also includes an Age Wall. It curves around one side of the site. The wall gets higher based on the ages of the victims. So, the wall starts at 3 inches tall at one end to represent 3-year-old Dana Falkenberg and rises to 71 inches to represent 71-year-old John Yamnicky.

The planned 9/11 Pentagon Memorial Visitor Education Center will be built near the memorial. There, interactive exhibits and special programs will explain the events of September 11, 2001, and highlight the stories of the victims and heroes.

The Flight 93 National Memorial

In 2005, the National Park Foundation began raising money to build a Flight 93 memorial at the crash site near Shanksville, Pennsylvania. The memorial was funded by individual donors, corporations,

In 2018, the Tower of Voices was built at the Flight 93 National Memorial.

and foundations. It opened in 2011. The Flight 93 National Memorial features a marble wall bearing the names of all 40 victims who died in the crash there. The Tower of Voices is a 93-foot (28 m) tower that contains 40 wind chimes, one for each victim. The tower is mathematically designed so that each wind chime produces a different musical note.

9/11 Memorial & Museum

Plans for a memorial at Ground Zero began soon after the attacks. In 2006, these plans stalled because of budget concerns. New York City mayor Michael Bloomberg stepped in to help. Bloomberg raised $450 million from donors to fund the memorial. Building the memorial took five years. It opened in 2011, on the tenth anniversary of the 9/11 terrorist attacks.

One artifact on display at the 9/11 Memorial Museum is the Survivors' Stairs. During the attacks, hundreds of survivors used this outdoor staircase to escape the WTC plaza.

The 9/11 Memorial features two square pools where the Twin Towers once stood. Waterfalls cascade down the inner walls of the pools. The names of those who died in the WTC attacks are inscribed around outer edges of the pools.

Architect Michael Arad designed the 9/11 Memorial. It is called *Reflecting Absence.*

Many people who survived the tower collapses or worked at the site during the rescue and cleanup phase died in later weeks, months, and years. This was because they developed illnesses from breathing in the smoke and toxic fumes at Ground Zero. In 2019, the Memorial Glade was installed at the 9/11 Memorial in their honor. The glade features six large granite stones along a pathway near the south pool.

In 2014, the 9/11 Memorial Museum opened. The museum is also located at the Ground Zero site, near the memorial pools. Its mission is to honor and remember the victims, victims' families, rescuers, and volunteers. The museum includes photos, stories, and artifacts from the 9/11 terrorist attacks and its aftermath.

Thousands of people visit the 9/11 Memorial & Museum each day. It offers guests a place to learn about and reflect on the events of 9/11. The museum's Family Room provides victims' families with a private space to remember their loved ones.

Many people who visit the 9/11 Memorial place small commemorative items on the edges of the pools near victims' inscribed names. Family members leave letters, photographs, stuffed animals, and other personal items by the names of their loved ones. Even strangers leave items in tribute. Each night, museum staff collects these items to store in the museum, ensuring they will be preserved.

The 9/11 WTC Memorial Quilt Project

Groups overseeing the landmarks and sites of the 9/11 terrorist attacks weren't the only ones organizing memorials of the events. In 2001, Amy Sue Leasure-Hedt started an art project to honor the 9/11 victims. Leasure-Hedt was an emergency dispatcher and quilter from Arizona. Shortly after the attacks, she created a website describing her idea. Leasure-Hedt wanted to make quilts in tribute to those who died in the 9/11 terrorist attacks. Her website had instructions for making a quilt square in red, white, and blue. She invited people to sew a square and donate it to her project.

Leasure-Hedt received more than 20,000 quilt squares from people in more than 30 countries. The squares honored victims from the WTC, the Pentagon, and Flight 93. Some also honored the police officers and firefighters who participated in rescuing victims. Leasure-Hedt had received more than enough squares to make 300 quilts. She organized groups of quilters around the country to help sew the quilts. Sadly, Leasure-Hedt died of cancer in 2002 before the quilts were completed.

After Leasure-Hedt's death, the project was on hold until Brian Kohler, a quilter from Seattle, Washington, started it up again. The quilts were completed in 2004 and put on display in Seattle. However, Kohler didn't have the time or resources to continue the exhibit. So after a few months, the quilts went into storage.

Beverly Kuemin had donated a square in 2001 and had traveled to Seattle to see the completed quilts. She contacted Kohler about displaying the quilts around the country. He sent the quilts to her in 2015 and she took over the responsibilities of exhibiting the 9/11 WTC Memorial Quilt Project. The nonprofit organization relies on donations to fund a traveling exhibit of the quilts. Kohler hopes that eventually the quilts will have a permanent home at a museum in New York City.

Another 9/11 memorial quilt has been on display inside the 9/11 Museum. It features an image of every victim of the attacks.

New York City Veterans' Services Commissioner Loree Sutton speaks at a gala held in New York City to mark the fifteenth anniversary of the 9/11 terrorist attacks. The gala included a silent auction to raise money for Tuesday's Children.

Chapter 7

9/11 CHARITIES TODAY

In the years after the attacks, many 9/11 charities shut down. Some lacked funding. Others had fulfilled their missions. For example, by 2011, many children had aged out of America's Camp. So, that year, the camp closed.

But some 9/11 charities and funds continue operating today. One is the Cantor Fitzgerald Relief Fund. In 2005, it expanded to help victims of other emergencies and natural disasters. Since then, the fund has raised hundreds of millions of dollars for these causes.

Tuesday's Children also expanded its mission. The charity still helps families affected by 9/11. However, it now also helps people around the world impacted by terrorism and violence. One way Tuesday's Children does this is through youth outreach programs. Each year, Tuesday's Children hosts the Project COMMON BOND camp. Like America's Camp, this program brings together young adults who lost family members to terrorism. But, Project COMMON BOND operates in countries all over the world.

In later years, new charities also emerged for victims of the 9/11 terrorist attacks. One was HEART 9/11. It was founded in 2007 by first responders who helped clean up and rebuild Ground Zero. HEART 9/11's mission is to help other communities across the United States rebuild after human-made or natural disasters. Since 2007, the organization's volunteers have helped rebuild several US cities after floods, hurricanes, and other tragic events.

September 11th Victim Compensation Fund

The VCF also evolved over time. The fund closed in 2004 after serving survivors, first responders, and victims' families. However, it was activated again in 2011 as part of the James Zadroga 9/11 Health and Compensation Act of 2010. The fund was named after James Zadroga, a New York City police officer who spent months working at Ground Zero. He was the first police officer whose death was directly linked to conditions he developed from working at the site.

But Zadroga was just one of many who developed illnesses from this exposure. Thousands of first responders, survivors, and cleanup crewmembers had gotten sick over the years after being exposed to toxic air at the crash sites in New York City; Washington, DC; and Pennsylvania. Illnesses victims developed included lung disease, heart disease, and cancer.

The Zadroga Act also created the World Trade Center Health Program. This program provides free medical care to tens of

In 2015, firefighters, police officers, and government officials lobbied the US Congress to extend the Zadroga Act. The act was first extended for five years. In 2019, it was extended again until 2090.

thousands of people living with 9/11-related illnesses. In addition to treating physical illnesses, the program also provides treatment for 9/11-related mental illnesses, such as post-traumatic stress disorder (PTSD).

9/11 Day

Events of 9/11 remembrance still continue today as well. The date of September 11 is commemorated each year by various events and organizations. One of these was founded by David Paine and Jay Winuk in 2002 in memory of Winuk's brother, Glenn. Glenn had worked as an attorney in

Jay Winuk (*left*) and David Paine speak at a 9/11 tribute event in 2009.

a building near the WTC. He was also a volunteer firefighter and paramedic. After evacuating his office on 9/11, Glenn rushed to the WTC to help survivors. He died when the South Tower collapsed.

In honor of Glenn's bravery and service, Winuk and Paine started a nonprofit organization called One Day's Pay in 2002. The name was later changed to MyGoodDeed. The organization's goal is to turn September 11 from a day of tragedy into a day of charity and service. Over the years, the nonprofit has organized several 9/11 Day charity events across the country. During these events, people perform acts of service in their communities. MyGoodDeed also provides free materials to US schools to educate children about the 9/11 terrorist attacks. And, since its founding, the nonprofit worked to have September 11 recognized as a national day of service.

In 2011, volunteers in Fort Meade, Maryland, helped build a playground for military children as part of the National Day of Service and Remembrance.

In September 2009, MyGoodDeed got its wish. President Barack Obama officially declared September 11 to be a National Day of Service and Remembrance. The president encouraged people to volunteer in honor of those affected by the 9/11 terrorist attacks. Since this founding, the National Day of Service and Remembrance has become the largest charitable day in the country. Each year, more than 15 million Americans observe the day by volunteering in their communities or donating to charities.

Forever United

The 9/11 terrorist attacks were the deadliest ever to occur on US soil. They shocked the nation and caused people around the globe to mourn. In the aftermath, people worldwide rallied behind victims, survivors, and first responders. Some donated money and supplies. Others spent long hours cleaning up at Ground Zero. And, some people helped simply by showing kindness to strangers. Each action, no matter how small, helped America heal.

The country has long since rebuilt from the destruction of September 11, 2001. However, there are still ways people help one another grow, heal, and remember. Each year, people across the country honor 9/11's heroes through acts of service and charity. Communities gather to hold candlelight vigils, memorial ceremonies, and moments of silence. And, people help keep the memory of 9/11's victims alive by donating to charities and memorial funds. These acts show that Americans will forever be united in remembering the 9/11 terrorist attacks.

TIMELINE

SEPTEMBER 11, 2001
Nearly 3,000 people are killed
and thousands more are injured
in the 9/11 terrorist attacks.

SEPTEMBER 13, 2001
Nino's Restaurant in New York
City opens its doors to serve
Ground Zero cleanup workers.

2001

2002

2002
America's Camp and the MyGoodDeed
organization are founded.

2007
HEART 9/11 is founded.

2005
The Cantor Fitzgerald Relief Fund expands to help victims of other emergencies and natural disasters.

2009
President Barack Obama makes September 11 a National Day of Service and Remembrance.

2011
America's Camp closes. The September 11th Victim Compensation Fund is revived under the James Zadroga 9/11 Health and Compensation Act of 2010.

2019
The Memorial Glade is dedicated at the 9/11 Memorial & Museum.

2014
The 9/11 Memorial Museum opens.

GLOSSARY

aftermath—the time immediately following a bad and usually destructive event.

artifact—an object remaining from a particular location or time period.

civilian—of or relating to something nonmilitary. A civilian is a person who is not an active member of the military.

commemorate—to honor and remember an important person or event. An instance of commemorating is a commemoration.

demolition—the act of destroying something, especially by using explosives.

discrimination—unfair treatment, often based on race, religion, or gender.

dispatcher—a person whose job is to send someone or something to a particular place for a particular purpose.

embassy—the residence and offices of an ambassador in a foreign country.

hijack—to take over by threatening violence.

Islam—the religion of Muslims as described in the Koran. Islam is based on the teachings of the god Allah through the prophet Muhammad.

landmark—an important structure of historical or physical interest.

memorial—something that serves to remind people of a person or an event.

monitor—to watch, keep track of, or oversee.

Muslim—a person who follows Islam.

nonprofit—not existing or carried on for the purpose of making a profit.

paramedic—someone trained to care for a patient before or during the trip to a hospital.

Pentagon—the five-sided building near Washington, DC, where the main offices of the US Department of Defense are located.

pharmacist—a person licensed to prepare and sell drugs.

post-traumatic stress disorder (PTSD)—a mental condition that can be caused by a very shocking or difficult experience. Symptoms of PTSD include depression and anxiety.

respirator—a mask worn over the nose and mouth that filters out dangerous substances from the air.

scholarship—money or aid given to help a student continue his or her studies.

vigil—a gathering during which people stay in place and quietly wait or pray.

violate—to take away or interfere with something in an unfair or illegal way.

ONLINE RESOURCES

Booklinks
NONFICTION NETWORK
FREE! ONLINE NONFICTION RESOURCES

To learn more about standing united after 9/11, please visit **abdobooklinks.com** or scan this QR code. These links are routinely monitored and updated to provide the most current information available.

INDEX